SELF

THE ...
PRACTICING SELF
LOVE AND
REALIZING THAT
YOU ARE ENOUGH

LEVESE WILLIAMS

Introduction

I want to thank you and congratulate you for purchasing this book, *"SELF LOVE: THE ART OF PRACTICING SELF LOVE AND REALIZING THAT YOU ARE ENOUGH."*

This book contains proven steps and strategies on how to develop self-love which is one of the cornerstones to happiness.

Do you know you are very special and you deserve love? In a century where hatred, violence, and chaos prevail, practicing self-love can be very challenging. In fact, our society has underrated self-love to a point where some individuals consider self-love an act of selfishness and narcissism.

In reality, self-love is about getting in touch with yourself, and focusing on your well-being and happiness. When you despise yourself, your self-esteem, and self-image shatters, which creates life obstacles.

To live a happier and healthier life, practicing self-love is as important as the ability to draw breath. Nevertheless, how do you practice self-love?

This book will show you how. In this guide, we shall outline 7 easy steps you can take towards practicing self-love. We shall talk about how self-love can help you accept yourself, and eliminate negative thoughts and limiting beliefs that hinder your progress and success. I hope that this book will provide some guidance on your journey. Thanks again for purchasing this book, I hope you enjoy it!

Thank you!

Table of Contents

Understanding Self-Love and Its Importance

Often, we understand how to love others as well as how to show compassion, admiration, and love towards them, but unfortunately, we do not know how to love ourselves. Self-love simply entails loving and accepting yourself as you are regardless of flaws and shortcomings.

Unfortunately, many of us confuse self-love with vanity, arrogance, egotism, and selfishness; however, in reality, self-love is about improving yourself by being compassionate, loving, and patient towards yourself.

To practice self-love, the first step is to understand its importance and value in your life.

Self-love helps you accept yourself

One of the biggest self-love misconceptions is that it causes you to overlook your flaws instead of aiming for self-improvement. However, only through self-love can you accept yourself, your flaws, and your shortcomings and work on them to become better. Moreover, when you love yourself, because you understand your self-worth, you do not feel the need to compare yourself to others.

Self-acceptance is a key characteristic of practicing self-love and it helps you to be more self-aware, which helps you to realize that you have unique qualities and traits.

Self-love improves your mental and physical health

Self-love is about practicing unconditional love towards yourself. When you fail to practice self-love, and choose to engage in negative self-talk, your physical and mental health is negatively affected.

The body produces a hormone called 'cortisol'. Cortisol concentration in the body increases when you experience constant stress. When cortisol increases, it places your body in a catabolic state that causes destruction of body cells. Cell destruction in turn causes muscle loss, bone loss, and a weak and easily compromised immune system. Moreover, high levels of cortisol make it hard to lose abdominal fat.

When you practice self-love, you help train your mind not to engage in negative self-talk and self-criticism; instead, you use self-assurances and positive self-talk to improve yourself.

For instance, if you are obese, through self-love, you learn to accept yourself and use positive thinking to lose weight rather than criticizing yourself. This positivity keeps you calm; when your body stays in a state of relaxation, your cortisol levels stay within normal range, which consequently, improves your health.

Self-love helps you tackle adversity

When you are going through a rough patch in life, it is beneficial to practice self-love and compassion towards yourself. A study conducted on recently divorced couples showed that those who practiced self-love bounced back more easily than those who criticized themselves.

When you are going through a rough patch, because you are upset and depressed, you may be more likely to criticize and blame yourself. However, practicing self-love may help you to remain strong enough to make it through these tough times. Telling yourself you deserve to be happy and good things will come your way is a more positive, self-loving way of dealing with adversity.

Self-love increases self-esteem and confidence

Self-esteem is the emotional assessment of your self-worth and value; self-esteem is directly linked to self-love. The more you love yourself, the higher your self-esteem and confidence will be.

When your self-esteem is low, you may degrade, demoralize, and devalue yourself because you believe you are not worthy of love. Moreover, because you view yourself as someone who is not worthy of love, you may find yourself not setting goals and achieving goals. Low self-esteem gives way to lack of confidence, which ultimately, negatively, affects your progress towards living a good life.

When you practice self-love, you re-affirm your self-worth and affection. Self-love helps you look past your insecurities, and revives your faith in your abilities and qualities. When you believe in yourself, it becomes easier to view yourself as worthy, which increases your self-esteem and confidence greatly.

Key Takeaway

An important element to changing from self-hatred and criticism is to understand how you stand to benefit from loving yourself unconditionally. Hopefully this chapter has given you some insight as to how you can benefit from loving yourself. In the following chapters we will cover steps on how to go about developing self-love.

Step 1: Admit Your Problem

It is common belief that the first step to recovery is admitting you have a problem. Hence, if you feel a lack of self-love in your life, you need to admit the problem and decide to face it head-on.

In our first step, we will discuss how you can confirm and validate personal feelings related to your lack of self-love.

Write it down

So now you have realized that you really do not love yourself, the first thing to you should do is write down all your feelings and emotions about yourself. When you write something down, it becomes harder to ignore or run from it. It becomes a real thing. Write down your current situation in a journal, as well as how you feel about yourself. Make this description as detailed as possible.

You can write adjectives, words, sentences, negative thoughts, and anything else that captures your current assessment of yourself. For instance, you can write the words that come to your mind when you think of yourself; these may include words such as weak, unconfident, gullible, selfish, or stupid.

What you write will depend on how you feel about yourself; writing everything on paper helps you discover your true feelings for yourself. When you discover the areas of self-love that you are lacking in, only then can you begin to change these negative thoughts and feelings for more positive self-assuring ones of love and positivity.

Also, as you write this personal assessment, allow the feelings of pain and anguish that you may experience. Allow them to move deeper because the more pain you feel, the more you can grieve and release it.

Describe the impact of your feelings

Once you have written how you feel about yourself, describe how your feelings and lack of self-love have impacted your life. How they have possibly made your life awful, impossible, unmanageable, and miserable. Think of all the circumstances, consequences, and mishaps you have faced due to your feelings.

For instance, lack of self-love may have alienated you from your friends, family, and society, or may have caused you to let go of your dreams because you do not consider yourself capable of achieving your goals.

It is very important to highlight all the problems a lack of self-love has caused in your life because when you do this, you realize how much you have missed. This realization motivates you to make changes.

Picture it

Once you have admitted the problem, another important thing to do is to picture how loving yourself would feel and what changes practicing self-love would bring into your life. This is important because when you visualize something, taking the necessary steps to reach your destination becomes easier.

For instance, picture a life where you practice unconditional love towards yourself: a life where you never let criticism become a constant. For instance, if you are in the habit of beating yourself up over tiny mistakes, reverse that scenario and picture yourself saying, *"This mistake has taught me a big lesson, I'm glad I love myself enough to let it go and improve myself so that I don't repeat the same mistake again."*

Consider how that makes you feel. Does the possibility of self-love liberate and open up your life and all the possibilities it has?

Once you have completed the first step, you can continue to the second step on your journey to bringing changes to your attitude and instilling self-love in your life.

Key Takeaway

Understanding your problem is the first step to change. Once you know you have a problem, you become more conscious and take the necessary steps to change.

Step 2: Cleanse Your Negative Thoughts

Your thoughts, whether they are positive or negative, shape your behavior and attitude. One main reason why you fail to love yourself is negative thoughts. Your self-talk or self-dialogue is the inner voice inside your head talking to you 24/7.

To practice self-love, **YOU MUST** practice positive self-talk. To practice positive self-talk, you need to mute your inner critic. To do that, you need to cleanse negative self-talk and thoughts.

Let us look at ways you can cleanse your negative thoughts.

Say it aloud

When cleansing your thoughts, the first thing you need to do is intently listen to what your inner voice says. If possible, write down all the negative chatter in your head and read it aloud.

It is said that a few celebrities are in the habit of reading aloud negative posts and tweets because according to them, it makes them see how absurd and ridiculous the comments truly are. Try this out with the voices inside your head.

For instance, if you feel not worthy of love because your partner cheated on you, say this aloud, laugh at the absurdity of your thought, and tell yourself you are not the reason for someone's weaknesses and you deserve to be loved by someone much better.

Although this strategy may sound hilariously silly, in reality, when you face your darkest thoughts and speak them aloud, you realize you were blaming yourself for something that was not your fault.

If laughing at your negative thoughts is difficult, call a friend and let him or her tell you that your thought is absurd and laugh along with you.

Challenge negative thoughts

Once you are aware of the negative thoughts inside your head, systematically challenge each one. This is the best way to cleanse negativity of your mind. To challenge negative thoughts, ask yourself the following questions:

1. Ask yourself what evidence is there for and against the negative thoughts. For instance, pick one negative thought such as *"I hate myself because I can't ever accomplish anything."*

Now, ask yourself, is there evidence to support or disprove this thought. If unemployment is what has led to this thinking, ask yourself if the reason for your unemployment is to find a better and more suitable job. If you have a stable job, then consider it as evidence against your negative thoughts.

2. Once you have evidence against your negative thoughts, ask yourself if you have been too quick to jump to conclusions. Make a mental note of not jumping to conclusions next time and always look for alternative explanations for your thoughts and actions.

Set a time limit

Just as important as it is to identify your negative thoughts, it is equally important not to dwell over them for long periods because that only strengthens your belief in them.

To cleanse negative thoughts, set a time limit for engaging in negative self-talk. For instance, set a time of 15 minutes each day from 5 p.m. to 5.15 p.m. to think about your negative thoughts and indulge in negative self-talk.

By doing this, you will keep yourself from spending too much time dwelling on negativities. Every time a negative thought pops into your head, tell it to wait for the time allocated for thoughts of its nature. When you postpone thoughts, many of them disappear and become less important.

For instance, if you are criticizing yourself because your boss just told you there was a slight mistake in your proposal, by postponing that thought, you will decrease its intensity and make it less upsetting. It might even slip out of your mind before the allocated 'negative thinking' time comes around.

To delay a negative thought, another interesting thing you can do is to stick out your tongue, poke your belly, or slap your wrist just as a negative thought enters your mind. You can find a body response that brings your mind back to the present moment.

Change your company

A major cause of negative self-talk is the company you keep. If you surround yourself with people who discourage you, blame you, and criticize you all the time, your negative self-talk will never convert into positive self-talk. Hence, it is essential to be in the company of those who shower you with unconditional love and those who encourage positive changes in your life.

If you have a friend who brings out your insecurities and always highlights the darker aspects of life, as much as possible, avoid this friend. Also, do not share your plan to practice self-love with such a 'friend' because it is likely he or she will try to push you off this path.

As you practice this step, you will feel the cloud of negativity lift from your mind and there will be clarity. In the next step, we will discuss how to use your newfound clarity to cultivate a positive mindset.

Key Takeaway

Before you can actually behave in a particular way, you have thought about that specific behavior. Thus, before you practice self-hate, you have actually criticized yourself and harbored negative thoughts. Learning how to get rid of these negative thoughts will create room for positive thoughts.

Step 3: Cultivate A Positive Mindset

Did you know that having a positive mind improves your health? According to one study, if you embrace positive thinking, your health also improves. We mention this to highlight the importance of cultivating a positive mindset. If a positive mindset can improve your health, what wonders could it do to for your self-esteem and self-worth?

When you engage in positive self-talk, you limit the time you spend ruminating on the past or criticizing yourself. Thinking positively gives you an opportunity to reflect on your qualities and accomplishments, which in turn, eliminates feelings of self-hatred.

To cultivate a positive mindset, practice the following:

Believe in the freedom of choice

The mistake we often make, a mistake that often gives way to negativity is forgetting to believe in the freedom of choice. The first thing you need to do to cultivate a positive mindset is to believe in the freedom of choice.

What this means is having the freedom to choose your belief and the thoughts you ruminate on. For instance, if someone says you are not worthy of love, whether you believe or dismiss this thought is your choice.

It is important to remember that the thoughts and belief you hold true about yourself and life create your reality. Create your reality by choosing to believe in your abilities and qualities rather than your flaws.

Practice positive self-talk

As discussed earlier, positive self-talk is the positive chatter inside your head; it is an essential part of practicing self-love. Once you have faith in your freedom of choice, switch from negative to positive self-talk.

Follow the steps below to practice positive self-talk:

1. If you have thoughts such as, *"I can't do this, or I will fail,"* change them to *"I can do it, or I will be successful."*

2. Use daily affirmations to remind yourself you are worthy of self-love. For instance, affirm yourself at least 20 times a day by saying, *"I am capable, I am enough, I choose to reach for better feelings, my life is unfolding beautifully, or each step I take is taking me to where I want to be."*

These affirmations will have a long-term effect on you; slowly, your mind will attach itself to these positive mantras.

3. Every night before you go to bed, acknowledge one good thing that happened to you during the day. This exercise helps you remember there are many good things around you, which gives way to positive thinking.

For instance, if an act of gratitude you practiced towards a stranger made that stranger smile, remember that and it will make you smile and bring you one step closer to loving yourself.

Focus on the good in life and be enthusiastic

To cultivate a positive mindset, focus on the good things in life rather than whining and complaining about the past, or how lacking your life is. When you focus on the good things in your life, no matter how small they are, you attract positivity towards your life.

For instance, if you have a job that does not pay well, focus on the aspect that you have a job rather than the fact that it does not pay well. You can do this by thinking about all the unemployed people who have no source of income. By doing this, your thoughts will automatically shift from focusing on the negative and start focusing on the positive.

Moreover, learn to be enthusiastic because enthusiastic people are generally enthusiastic about life. When you are enthusiastic, you maintain the attitude that life is good, and you are fortunate to be alive. You can increase enthusiasm by doing things you love and pursuing your passion, something we shall talk about in the next step.

Key Takeaway

Once you develop a positive mindset, loving yourself becomes much easier because you understand that you are worthy of love despite your successes and your shortcomings.

Step 4: Pursue Your Passions

At one point or another, each of us experiences situations that bring us down. These are instance where we feel as if nothing we do is good enough, and it seems as if everyone has a better personality, better job, better appearance, and better life. More often than not, these feelings do not last long and are just a blip on your radar, but sometimes, these feeling prolong their stay and affect your self-esteem.

When you experience low self-esteem, loving yourself, changing your thinking and behavioral patterns becomes impossible; when you hate yourself, you detach from your authentic self and forget who you are, what you value, and what you want in life.

Dr. Phil has a beautiful quote that sums up the importance of finding your authentic self and in turn, loving yourself. He says, *"Your authentic self is who you are when you have no fear of judgment, or before the world starts pushing you around and telling you who you are supposed to be."*

This simply means when you act and behave like the person you are 'supposed' to be, as opposed to who you truly are, it is hard to love yourself because you do not know the self you are trying to love.

To find your authentic self, seek, and pursue your passions because when you work towards your passion, it brings you inner wisdom and a new level of self-awareness that allows you to understand and love yourself.

Let us find out how you can seek and pursue your passion.

Learn more about yourself

When finding your life's passion, the first thing you need to do is learn as much as you can about yourself. Perform the following exercise to learn about yourself.

1. Start by doing a personality assessment test and take a skills inventory because this will offer you insight into your traits and aptitudes. For instance, write about your personality traits such as generous, adventure seeker, curious, compassionate, or rebellious.

2. Next, ask yourself a number of questions that dig deeper into your likes and dislikes. For instance, ask yourself which activities make you the happiest. What natural skills do you possess that you value the most? Is there something you love doing so much that you lose track of time while doing it? What were your childhood dreams and goals? If you did not have people to worry about, or financially support your family, what would you be doing?

Write down all these questions, their answers, and thoroughly go through them so you get an idea of what you want in life.

If this practice reveals your job is just a way of earning money or pleasing people, consider gradual changes because you can never fully enjoy yourself and be completely happy if you are doing something for the sake of money or people. You will always feel unfulfilled and unhappy.

Go after your dreams

Once you have a thorough understanding of what you want and what makes you happy, do not hesitate to reach for it. If you spend your life worrying about what people will think, you will remain stuck in regret. Hence, to practice self-love, go after your dreams without fear of judgment and failure.

To go after your dreams, wholeheartedly commit to the pursuit; otherwise, you will leave space for fear and doubt. When you fully commit to a new dream, whether that dream is a career change, a relationship, or a healthier lifestyle, achieving that dream becomes easier.

For instance, if you discover your passion is traveling the world and becoming a tour guide, fully commit to this dream. Do not let doubt creep in by thinking, *"What if I run out of money, or what if I fail."*

Moreover, remember there is no such thing as failure, there is only feedback. This means that failure is nothing more than perception; you decide how you view it. When you start to believe failure does not exist, you do not hesitate to move towards your dreams no matter how impossible it seems. Even if you face challenges and you make mistakes, view them as lessons that help you improve yourself.

Finding and pursuing your passion will change your life outlook and you will start loving yourself because you will realize that doing what you love is what makes you a better and happier person.

Key Takeaway

Pursuing your passion is the first step to showing yourself how much you love yourself because you will now be doing things that you actually love. This step also shows that you love yourself enough to do something that you enjoy.

Step 5: Embrace Self-Forgiveness

Have you ever made a mistake that hurt your parents? Did you find it hard to sleep, eat, and work until they forgave you? If yes, you know the power of guilt and the importance of forgiveness.

In the fifth step, we will discuss how you can forgive yourself because until you do, you will never eliminate the guilt you carry for hurting yourself and you will continue to hate yourself.

How to Forgive Yourself

Everett L. Worthington Jr., a professor of psychology, says, *"A lot of people struggle with self-condemnation or self-blame because they've either done something they feel was wrong and they feel guilty, or because they feel that they're wrong or defective in some way and they feel a sense of shame."*

Your struggle can be one of these two; you eliminate the guilt and forgive yourself in the following way:

1. To forgive yourself, the first thing to do is to remind yourself that everyone makes mistakes. Moreover, tell yourself that just like everyone else, you are worthy of forgiveness.

2. Next, pick a mistake you have not forgiven yourself for the longest time and forgive yourself for it.

For instance, if you hate yourself because you made a snide comment about financially supporting your family, begin by asking for forgiveness. The likelihood is that they have forgiven you, but hearing it from them will reassure you and make it easier for you to forgive yourself.

If you still have trouble forgiving yourself, remind yourself that you are a good person and you did not mean to hurt anyone, it was a moment of weakness that has long passed.

3. To forgive yourself, another interesting thing you can practice is to recall the hurt a situation caused and give yourself the empathy you would give someone in a similar situation.

You can create a forgiveness ritual by writing yourself a letter and apologizing to yourself. This will help you visualize your mistake from another perspective, which will make forgiving yourself easier. While writing the letter, be as descriptive as possible, and explicitly explain your feelings. The more your feelings come out in the open, the lighter you will feel inside.

4. Because now you can forgive yourself, promise yourself never to repeat the same mistake again because if you ask forgiveness and repeat the same mistake, next time, seeking forgiveness will not be so easy.

Once you have embraced self-forgiveness, you will no longer feel guilt and hatred towards yourself.

Key Takeaway

Just as you forgive others when they wrong you, learn not to be too hard on yourself and forgive yourself too because you can never truly love yourself if you hold grudges, are ashamed and embarrassed of what you did.

Step 6: Make Lifestyle Changes

You must be wondering how a change to your lifestyle can help you love yourself. Well, it is simple; when you lead a healthy lifestyle, it improves your physical as well as emotional well-being. Practicing self-love is not possible if diseases such as anxiety and depression plague your body.

To improve your physical and mental health, implement the following lifestyle changes.

Diet

Your brain is responsible for your thoughts and emotional responses; thus, what you feed your body and brain affects your mood. This is the reason why a healthy and well balanced diet is important for physical health and your emotional well-being.

Moreover, studies show that eating healthy directly influences your emotional well-being and happiness; when you are happy, loving yourself becomes easier. To uplift your mood, there are certain foods you must avoid and certain foods you should add to your diet. These include:

Caffeine: If your daily caffeine intake is high, cut down your consumption of high caffeine drinks such as coffee, sodas, and tea. Caffeine is a stimulant that stimulates the body by increasing mental and physical functioning, which ends up increasing anxiety. Hence, if you drink coffee three to four times a day, bring this down to once a day.

Sugar: Increased sugar intake gives you temporary high but also causes rapid mood swings that can lead to anxiety. When you are anxious, you deny yourself the opportunity to think positively, work on your mistakes, forgive yourself, and accept yourself. Therefore, limit the amount of sugar you consume and instead, focus on eating healthy food.

Healthy Foods: Add whole grain foods such as legumes, beans, carrots, oats and sweet potatoes to your diet because these foods lower your blood sugar levels and limit sudden spikes in your sugar level. Additionally, eat foods such as fish, spinach, and avocado because these foods are rich in magnesium. Magnesium helps the brain produce serotonin; serotonin improves your mood and gives you energy.

Exercise

Exercise helps the brain produce serotonin and as discussed, serotonin uplifts your mood. Make a habit of exercising at least 15 minutes a day. You can join a gym or you can invest in a treadmill that allows you to workout at home. If you can manage it, a morning run is very beneficial to your health. If you make exercise a habit, you will feel energetic throughout the day.

Key takeaway

These simple lifestyle changes will allow you to practice self-care, which will help you realize you are enough and worthy.

Step 7: Celebrate and Reward Yourself

Are you familiar with 14 February? Of course, 14 February is a day of celebrating your love for the ones you love. It is a great day that has a great theme because you show someone how special he or she is and reward him or her for all he or she does for you.

Let us apply the same concept and find ways to celebrate, reward, and love yourself. However, do not confine this practice to once a year; make it a regular habit because celebrating and rewarding yourself is a way of practicing self-love.

Celebrating Yourself

Here is how you can celebrate yourself:

1. When going over the past week and remembering something awesome you did, give yourself a pat on the back. For instance, if you helped an old woman cross the road, appreciate yourself for this act of kindness and make a mental note to repeat it.

2. Create a list of things you like about yourself such as your generosity, kindness, humbleness, and honesty. No one else is going to see this list, do not be shy, and openly discuss your qualities

3. We often dwell on the negative things someone said to us or about us. Now is the time to remember a compliment you received. For instance, if your boss complimented you for a job well done you on a recent presentation, remember that compliment and allow yourself to feel awesome.

4. Everyone feels good when he or she is all dressed up. Today, dress up for no particular reason and let yourself feel good. If dressing up for no reason sounds silly to you, throw yourself a party by playing your favorite music and dancing to it. If your idea of a party is to binge-watch your favorite television show, then grab some popcorn and enjoy yourself; do this while looking dashing.

5. Reward yourself by taking yourself shopping and buying something you have not bought yourself because you did not think you were worthy of having it. For instance, if you have been meaning to buy an expensive perfume you love and have not bought it because you would rather spend the money on someone important, then quit such thinking and remember, there is no one as important as you are.

6. Another way to reward yourself is to draw yourself a hot bath. Start by infusing the bathwater with lavender oil or any oil that has a pleasing scent. Use bath salts of your choice and enjoy a long hot bath. Rewarding yourself with self-care is an essential part of increasing self-love.

Implement these fun and enjoyable practices in your life and soon, you will fall in love with yourself. Of course, you can do anything else you find rewarding and relaxing to enjoy and celebrate yourself.

Key Takeaway

Thus, far you are doing well; take a moment to reward yourself because this will give you the motivation to keep going.

Conclusion

Thank you again for purchasing this book!

We have just covered several steps that will help to guide you on your way to Self-love. Remember this is not just a destination but a constant journey. We should be always improving and seeking to become a better version ourselves all the while loving ourselves during the process. Remember that you are important, and furthermore, you are more than enough! I hope that this book has given you some insight and tips on how to love yourself unconditionally.

Follow the steps discussed in this book and you will notice the changes it will bring into your life. As you walk the path to self-love, I wish you all the best.

Finally, if you enjoyed this book, would you be kind enough to leave a review for this book on Amazon?

Thank you!

Self-Discipline: Developing Self Discipline Is The Key To Achieving Your Goals And Living Your Best Life

Understanding Self-Discipline

Self-discipline is the ability to control desires, impulses, behavior, and emotions. It is making the conscious decision to delay instant gratification or immediate pleasure in order to obtain long-term fulfillment and satisfaction. Self-discipline is about doing what is necessary now in order to achieve future goals.

You are self-disciplined if you have the ability to execute your game plan and take action regardless of discomforts or obstacles that may come your way. Self-discipline sometimes involves stepping outside of your comfort zone and doing things that need to be done at that moment whether you feel like it or not. Being self-disciplined does not means constantly living a life full of restrictions and limitations or giving up on everything you consider fun. It simply means making deliberate choices that keep you on track to achieving your goals instead of allowing impulsive actions to push you further away from what you really want to accomplish long term.

Benefits of Being Self-Disciplined

Self-discipline is an essential life skill that will help you succeed by helping you:

Stay Focused: Being self-disciplined helps you stay focused on your goals, work towards their accomplishment, and avoid distractions that may keep you from accomplishing your goals.

Earn Respect: First, self-discipline is not always an easy to cultivate habit and not everyone is; therefore, when you are self-disciplined, you command respect. For instance, if you are an always-on-time employee who completes his or her projects within the set deadlines, you may earn your employer's respect as well as coworkers and others you may want to work with. You will be seen as a person who gets things done.

Stay Active: Self-discipline helps you to consistently do the things necessary to maintain a healthy and positive body and mind. This helps to maintain a positive attitude and spirit which allows you to make better choices and helps maintain self-confidence.

Build Good Relationships: When you are in control of your words and your behavior, people see you as someone who is dependable and trustworthy. They see you as someone they would like to be around; someone they would like to know. Building good relationships helps you to accomplish your goals and also help others accomplish their goals.

Get Things Done and Be Happy: Being self-disciplined helps you avoid distractions, which in turn helps you to finish work faster and more effectively. This leads to peace of mind and inner happiness. One of the keys to feeling successful is making progress towards your goals. When you set a goal and make measurable progress towards that goal you feel a sense of accomplishment and satisfaction. Self-discipline helps you to develop the character of a person who does what they say they will do.

Stay Stress/Tension Free: Self-discipline helps you to complete tasks on time or in advance, which eliminates the fear or anxiety of an unknown outcome or a situation. For instance, when you study well for an exam, or execute your work in a timely manner, you help to decrease some possible stress.

Improved Self-Esteem: Just as your value increases to others when you practice self-discipline, your value to yourself increases as well. You too see yourself as capable of making things happening. This helps you to feel good about yourself thereby increasing your self-esteem. As you accomplish more and more you gain confidence and are more assured of yourself and your capabilities.

Now that we have covered the importance of self-discipline, and the various benefits that come along with being self-disciplined, let us look at a systematic way to cultivate self-discipline.

Thank you.

Printed in Great Britain
by Amazon

60038311R00031